DOVER · THRIFT · EDITIONS

Mother
A Book of Quotations

EDITED BY

HERB GALEWITZ

DOVER PUBLICATIONS, INC.
Mineola, New York

DOVER THRIFT EDITIONS

GENERAL EDITOR: PAUL NEGRI
EDITOR OF THIS VOLUME: HERB GALEWITZ

Bibliographical Note

Mother: A Book of Quotations is a new work, first published by Dover Publications, Inc., in 2002.

Library of Congress Cataloging-in-Publication Data

Mother : a book of quotations / edited by Herb Galewitz.
 p. cm. — (Dover thrift editions)
 ISBN 0-486-41940-1 (pbk.)
 1. Mothers—Quotations, maxims, etc. I. Galewitz, Herb. II. Series.

PN6084.M6 M63 2002
306.874'3—dc21

2001047368

Manufactured in the United States of America
Dover Publications, Inc., 31 East 2nd Street, Mineola, N.Y. 11501

Note

The mother-child relationship is paradoxical and, in a sense, tragic. It requires the most intense love on the mother's side, yet this very love must help the child grow away from the mother, and to become fully independent.

<div align="right">ERICH FROMM</div>

To the best of her ability, a mother guides her child through infancy, childhood, and adolescence, providing him or her all the while with unconditional love and support. While she may not be perfect, a mother generously offers understanding as she nurtures the confidence and independence her child will need to survive. The special bond that exists between mother and child is a fluid one, resilient enough to withstand many inevitable changes. With patience, love, and a little luck, a mother takes great pride in the adult her child has become, and experiences the joy of watching this precious relationship develop into one of mutual respect, admiration, and affection.

This book is a loving appreciation of all the countless things mothers do in helping a child to reach a physical, emotional, and spiritual maturity. From the sweet and sentimental to the critical and analytical, the quotations in this book are a testament to the often complicated emotions that one feels toward mothers. Included in this thoughtful collection are proverbs and traditional sayings from around the world, insightful comments about motherhood in American society, and several quotations about mothers-in-law and grandmothers. The quotations are arranged alphabetically by author.

Did you ever hear of a great and good man who had not a good mother?

JOHN ADAMS

❧

Don't aim to be an earthly Saint, with eyes fixed on a star,
Just try to be the fellow that your mother thinks you are.

WILL S. ADKIN

❧

Where there is a mother in the house, matters speed well.

AMOS BRONSON ALCOTT

❧

". . . What do girls do who haven't any mothers to help them through their troubles?"

LOUISA MAY ALCOTT

❧

Mary was that Mother mild.
Jesus Christ her little Child.

CECIL FRANCES ALEXANDER

Before a day was over,
Here comes the rover,
For mother's kiss,—sweeter this
Than any other thing!

WILLIAM ALLINGHAM

?&

When by my bed I saw my mother kneel,
And with her blessing took her nightly kiss;
Whatever time destroys, he cannot this;—
E'en now that nameless kiss I feel.

WASHINGTON ALLSTON

?&

The ideal which the wife and mother makes for herself, the manner in which she understands duty and life, contain the fate of the community.

HENRI F. AMIEL

?&

To describe my mother would be to write about a hurricane in its perfect power.

MAYA ANGELOU

?&

When it comes to love, Mom's the word.

Bigamy is a crime for which the extreme penalty is two mothers-in-law.

Mother's Day comes nine months after Father's Day.

ANONYMOUS

Mothers are fonder of their children than their fathers, for they remember the pain of bringing them forth, and are surer that they are their own.

ARISTOTLE

❧

The crying need of the world is mental mothers. Primitive, physical, passionate mothers we have in abundance. But the mothers we need, the mothers who are to stimulate mentally the town, family, and church are all too rare.

FRANK R. ARNOLD

❧

The joys of parents are secret: and so are the griefs and fears.

FRANCIS BACON

❧

To be told that mother love is not an innate impulse but a free choice, a gift that can be given and withdrawn at will, confronts each of us with the fearsome possibility that we might have been born into a void of indifference.

ELISABETH BADINTER

❧

Instant availability without continuous presence is probably the best role a mother can play.

LOTTE BAILYN

❧

The heart of a mother is a deep abyss at the bottom of which you will always find forgiveness.

Husbands . . . know that all they have to do is to confront their own mother with their wife's and they will be found to neutralize one another.

A wife should not be allowed to go alone to see her mother.

Maternity begins in the imagination.

HONORÉ DE BALZAC

કે

For when you looked into my mother's eyes you knew, as if He had told you, why God sent her into the world—it was to open the minds of all who looked to beautiful thoughts.

JAMES M. BARRIE

કે

My wife is the kind of girl who'll not go anywhere without her mother, and her mother will go anywhere.

JOHN BARRYMORE

કે

The future of society is in the hands of the mothers. If the world was lost through woman, she alone can save it.

DE BEAUFORT

કે

When God thought of MOTHER, He must have laughed with satisfaction, and framed it quickly,—so rich, so deep, so divine, so full of soul, power, and beauty, was the conception.

The mother's heart is the child's schoolroom.

What the mother sings to the cradle goes all the way down to the coffin.

<div align="right">HENRY WARD BEECHER</div>

<div align="center">❧</div>

To a child's ear, "mother" is magic in any language.

<div align="right">ARLENE BENEDICT</div>

<div align="center">❧</div>

He maketh the barren woman to keep house; and to be a joyful mother of children.

A wise son maketh a glad father: but a foolish son is the heaviness of his mother.

Honour thy father and thy mother; that thy days may be long in the land which the Lord thy God giveth there.

Can a woman forget her sucking child, that she should not have compassion on the son of her womb? yea, they may forget.

Go not empty unto thy mother-in-law.

Despise not thy mother when she is old.

Her children arise up and call her blessed.

As is the mother, so is the daughter.

<div align="right">THE BIBLE</div>

<div align="center">❧</div>

A smart mother makes often a better diagnosis than a poor doctor.

<div align="right">AUGUST BIER</div>

The best thing that could happen to motherhood already has. Fewer women are going into it.

VICTORIA BILLINGS

ε∂

Every nursing mother, in the midst of her little dependent brood, has far more right to whine, sulk or scold, as temperament dictates, because beefsteak and coffee are not prepared for her and exactly to her taste, than any man ever had or ever can have during the present stage of human evolution.

ANTOINETTE BROWN BLACKWELL

ε∂

My mother groan'd! my father wept.
Into the dangerous world I lept!
Helpless, naked, piping loud,
Like a fiend hid in a cloud.

WILLIAM BLAKE

ε∂

When a woman is twenty, a child deforms her; when she is thirty, he preserves her; and when forty, he makes her young again.

LÉON BLUM

ε∂

I take a very practical view of raising children. I put a sign in each of their rooms: "Checkout Time is 18 years."

It is not until you become a mother that your judgment slowly turns to compassion and understanding.

ERMA BOMBECK

I have reached the age when a woman begins to perceive that she is growing into the person she least plans to resemble: her mother.

ANITA BROOKNER

The sweetest sounds to mortals given
Are heard in Mother, Home and Heaven.

WILLIAM GOLDSMITH BROWN

What art can a woman be good at? Oh, vain!
What art *is* she good at, but hurting her breast
With the milk-teeth of babes, and a smile at the pain?

Womanliness means only motherhood;
All love begins and ends there.

A mother who boasts two boys was ever accounted rich.

Women know
The way to rear up children (to be just)
They know a simple, merry, tender knack
Of tying sashes, fitting baby-shoes,
And stringing pretty words that make no sense . . .

ELIZABETH BARRETT BROWNING

Under Providence, I attribute any little distinction which I may have acquired in the world to the blessing which He conferred upon me in granting me such a mother.

JAMES BUCHANAN

The concept of "Momism" is male nonsense. It is the refuge of a man seeking excuses for his own lack of virility.

Some are kissing mothers and some are scolding mothers, but it is love just the same, and most mothers kiss and scold together.

PEARL S. BUCK

❧

Nature's loving proxy, the watchful mother.

EDWARD GEORGE BULWER-LYTTON

❧

In the mind of a woman, to give birth to a child is the short cut to omniscience.

GELETT BURGESS

❧

Peter remained on friendly terms with Christ notwithstanding Christ's having healed his mother-in-law.

SAMUEL BUTLER

❧

Lo! at the couch where infant beauty sleeps,
Her silent watch the mournful mother keeps;
She, while the lovely babe unconscious lies,
Smiles on her slumbering child with pensive eyes.

CAMPBELL

Give me the life of the boy whose mother is nurse, seamstress, washerwoman, cook, teacher, angel and saint, all in one, and whose father is guide, exemplar, and friend. No servants to come between. These are the boys who are born to the best fortune.

ANDREW CARNEGIE

How could Jimmy criticize me? I am his momma.

LILLIAN CARTER, *mother of former president Jimmy Carter*

A mother alone knows what it is to love and be happy.

CHAMISSO

The evil-hearted Grocer
 Would call his mother "Ma'am,"
And bow at her and bob at her,
 Her aged soul to damn.

I remember my mother, the day that we met,
 A thing I shall not entirely forget;
And I toy with the fancy that, young as I am,
 I should know her again if we met in a tram.

She was maintaining the prime truth of woman, the universal mother: that if a thing is worth doing, it is worth doing badly.

G. K. CHESTERTON

A man may compass important enterprises, he may become famous . . . he may deserve a measure of popular approval, but he is not right at heart, and can never be truly great, if he forgets his mother.

GROVER CLEVELAND

ঌ

Praise the child and you make love to the mother.

WILLIAM COBBETT

ঌ

Why do grandparents and grandchildren get along so well? They have the same enemy—the mother.

CLAUDETTE COLBERT

ঌ

Mother of God! no lady thou:
Common woman of common earth!

MARY ELIZABETH COLERIDGE

ঌ

So for the mother's sake the child was dear,
And dearer was the mother for the child.

SAMUEL TAYLOR COLERIDGE

Those love children always suffer because their mothers have crushed them under their stays trying to hide them, mores the pity. Yet, after all, a lovely unrepentant creature, big with child, is not such an outrageous sight.

<div align="right">COLETTE</div>

&

There can be no proper observation of a birthday which forgets the mother.

<div align="right">CALVIN COOLIDGE</div>

&

> Hundreds of dewdrops to greet the dawn,
> Hundreds of bees in the purple clover,
> Hundreds of butterflies on the lawn,
> But only one mother the wide world over.

<div align="right">GEORGE COOPER</div>

&

I know a mother-in-law who sleeps in her spectacles, the better to see her son-in-law suffer in her dreams.

<div align="right">ERNEST COQUELIN</div>

&

Better the child should cry than the mother sigh.

A rich child often sits in a poor mother's lap.

<div align="right">DANISH PROVERB</div>

The female of one of the emus, as soon as she catches sight of her progeny, becomes violently agitated, and notwithstanding the resistance of the father, appears to use her utmost endeavors to destroy them.

CHARLES DARWIN

Men compete with their sons, but mothers devour their daughters.

LEN DEIGHTON

There are times when parenthood seems nothing but feeding the mouth that bites you.

A suburban mother's role is to deliver children; obstetrically once and by car forever after.

PETER DE VRIES

I think it must somewhere be written, that the virtues of mothers shall be visited on their children, as well as the sins of the fathers.

CHARLES DICKENS

I never had a mother. I suppose a mother is one to whom you hurry when you are troubled.

EMILY DICKINSON

I think we're seeing in working mothers a change from "Thank God, it's Friday" to "Thank God, it's Monday." If any working

mother has not experienced that feeling, her children are not adolescent.

ANN DIEHL

ᐓ

Cleaning your house while your kids are still growing is like shoveling the walk before it stops snowing.

PHYLLIS DILLER

I want a girl just like the girl that married dear old dad.

WILLIAM DILLON

ᐓ

Just about the time a woman thinks her job is done, she becomes a grandmother.

EDWARD H. DRESCHNACK

ᐓ

No mother more indulgent but the true.

DRYDEN

ᐓ

With what a price we pay for the glory of motherhood.

ISADORA DUNCAN

ᐓ

I believe that always, or almost always, in all childhoods and in all the lives that follow them, the mother represents madness. Our mothers always remain the strangest, craziest people we've ever met.

MARGUERITE DURAS

The fact that we are all trained to be mothers from infancy on means that we are all trained to devote our lives to men, whether they are our sons or not; that we are all trained to force other women to exemplify the lack of qualities which characterizes the cultural construct of femininity.

<div align="right">ANDREA DWORKIN</div>

꙳

Most of the fellows in our neighborhood think a fellow should not go steady until he can tie his bow tie without his Mom's help.

<div align="right">EAGLE (MOULTON, TEXAS NEWSPAPER)</div>

꙳

There's nothing like an afternoon nap to refresh a young mother. At the end of it she has accomplished lots of work she couldn't have done if the youngster had been awake.

<div align="right">EAGLE (MURRAY, UTAH NEWSPAPER)</div>

꙳

What is home without a mother?

My mother was the making of me.

<div align="right">THOMAS ALVA EDISON</div>

꙳

Take motherhood: nobody ever thought of putting it on a moral pedestal until some brash feminists pointed out, about a century ago, that the pay is lousy and the career ladder is non-existent.

<div align="right">BARBARA EHRENREICH</div>

The mother of the year should be a sterilized woman with two adopted children.

<div align="right">PAUL EHRLICH</div>

<div align="center">える</div>

The mother's yearning, that completest type of the life in another life which is the essence of real human love, feels the presence of the cherished child even in the base degraded man.

Life began with waking up and loving my mother's face.

<div align="right">GEORGE ELIOT</div>

<div align="center">える</div>

The mother is the child's supreme parent.

<div align="right">HAVELOCK ELLIS</div>

<div align="center">える</div>

There was never a child so lovely but his mother was glad to get him asleep.

Men are what their mothers made them.

<div align="right">RALPH WALDO EMERSON</div>

<div align="center">える</div>

The good mother saith not, "Will you?" but gives.

A child may have too much of his mother's blessing.

<div align="center">He that would the daughter win,
Must with the mother first begin.</div>

<div align="right">ENGLISH PROVERB</div>

For a short while, our mothers' bodies are the boundaries and personal geography which are all that we know of the world. Once we no longer live beneath our mother's heart, it's the earth with which we form the same dependent relationship.

LOUISE ERDRICH

It is safer in a mother's lap than in a lord's bed.

ESTONIAN PROVERB

I warned my son against taking home the foal of a bad mother.

EURIPIDES

If a writer has to rob his mother, he will not hesitate. The "Ode On a Grecian Urn" is worth any number of old ladies.

WILLIAM FAULKNER

Motherhood is never honored by excessive talk about the heroics of pregnancy.

LEONARD FEENEY

Mother Knows Best.

EDNA FERBER

An infant, when her love first came—
A man, I find it just the same;
Reverently I breathe her name,
　　The blessed name of mother.

<div align="right">GEORGE GRIFFITH FETTER</div>

છ

Nobody knows of the lessons taught
　Of loving one another;
Nobody knows of the patience sought,
　Nobody—only mother.

<div align="right">THE FIRESIDE</div>

છ

A mother is not a person to lean on but a person to make leaning unnecessary.

<div align="right">DOROTHY CANFIELD FISHER</div>

છ

The mother cult is something that will set future generations roaring with laughter.

<div align="right">GUSTAVE FLAUBERT</div>

છ

. . . a friend can't take a mother's place. I need my mother as an example which I can follow. I want to be able to respect her.

<div align="right">ANNE FRANK</div>

First, every woman, I don't care who she is, prefers her son to her husband. . . . And why shouldn't she prefer someone who is so much like herself, who represents nine months of special concern and love and intense physical closeness—someone she actually created?

IAN FRAZIER

The truth is that it is not the sins of the fathers that descend unto the third generation, but the sorrows of the mothers.

MARILYN FRENCH

A man who has been the indisputable favorite of his mother keeps for life the feeling of a conqueror, that confidence of success that often induces real success.

SIGMUND FREUD

Strangely, many mothers who loved their daughters—and mine was one—did not want their daughters to grow up like them either. They knew we needed something more.

BETTY FRIEDAN

Mother is food; she is love; she is warmth; she is earth. To be loved by her means to be alive, to be rooted, to be at home.

Mother's love is peace. It need not be acquired, it need not be deserved.

The mother-child relationship is paradoxical and, in a sense, tragic. It requires the most intense love on the mother's side, yet

this very love must help the child grow away from the mother, and to become fully independent.

<div align="right">ERICH FROMM</div>

❧

A mother takes twenty years to make a man of her boy, and another woman makes a fool of him in twenty minutes.

> Home is the place where, when you have to go there,
> They have to take you in.

<div align="right">ROBERT FROST</div>

❧

The Mother-in-Law remembers not, that she was a Daughter-in-Law.

Everyone can keep house better than her Mother, till she trieth.

<div align="right">THOMAS FULLER</div>

❧

Do you think your mother and I should have liv'd comfortably so long together, if ever we had been married?

<div align="right">JOHN GAY</div>

❧

> You may have tangible wealth untold;
> Caskets of jewels and coffers of gold.
> Richer than I you can never be—
> I had a mother who read to me.

<div align="right">STRICKLAND GILLILAN</div>

The mother as a social servant instead of a home servant will not lack in true mother duty. . . . From her work, loved and honored though it is, she will return to the home life, the child life, with an eager, ceaseless pleasure, cleansed of all the fret and faction and weariness that so mar it now.

It is not motherhood that keeps the housewife on her feet from dawn to dusk; it is the house service, not child service.

When we see great men and women, we give credit to their mothers. When we see inferior men and women—and that is a common circumstance—no one presumes to the question of the motherhood that has produced them.

Maternal instinct, merely as an instinct, is unworthy of our superstitious reverence.

You cannot teach every mother to be a good school educator or a good college educator. Why should we expect every mother to be a good nursery educator?

> So when the great word "Mother!" rang once more,
> I saw at last its meaning and its place;
> Not the blind passion of the brooding past,
> But Mother—the World's Mother—come at last,
> To love as she had never loved before—
> To feed and guard and teach the human race.

You may observe mother instinct at its height in a fond hen sitting on china eggs—instinct, but no brains.

If love, devotion to duty, sublime self-sacrifice, were enough in child-culture, mothers would achieve better results; but there is another requisite too often lacking—knowledge.

CHARLOTTE PERKINS GILMAN

Don't go in the lion's cage tonight, mother darling,
For the lions are ferocious as can be.

JOHN GILROY

જ

Girls often marry men who remind them of their fathers.
Maybe that explains all the crying by mothers.

GLOBE (ATCHISON, KANSAS NEWSPAPER)

જ

Every boy who has a dog should also have a mother, so the dog
will be fed regularly.

GLOBE (NORTH DAKOTA NEWSPAPER)

જ

It's not easy being a mother. If it were, fathers would do it.

THE GOLDEN GIRLS (T.V. SHOW)

જ

What do you do with all the antennae of motherhood when
they become obsolete? What do you do with the loose wires that
dangle after eighteen years of intimate connection to your own
child? What use is there for the expertise of motherhood that
took so long to acquire?

There is no shower for a woman when she completes the
trimester of her life spent as a full-time mother. There is no mid-
wife to help that woman deliver a healthy adult.

ELLEN GOODMAN

Lullaby, lullaby, thy mother is coming back
From the laurels by the river,
From the sweet banks she will bring thee flowers
All sorts of Flowers, roses and scented pinks.

GREEK LULLABY

❧

As well as her love for her child then, there exists in every mother an aversion for the child . . . If you recognize mother love, do you also recognize mother hate?

GEORG GRODDECK

❧

Love is a roller coaster. Motherhood is a whole amusement park.

CATHY GUISEWITE

❧

There is no influence so powerful as that of the mother, but next in rank in efficacy is that of schoolmaster.

SARAH JOSEPHA HALE

❧

A woman has two smiles that an angel might envy—the smile that accepts a lover before words are uttered, and the smile that lights on the first born babe, and assures it of a mother's love.

THOMAS C. HALIBURTON

❧

You shall not take him, I care nothing for honour. I care only for the child that my womb has held, that my pain has brought

forth, that my breasts have nourished. I care nothing for your wars. He was born of love; shall the blossom of love be destroyed by your hatreds?

<div align="right">RADCLYFFE HALL</div>

◈

I find, by close observation, that the mothers are the levers which move in education. The men talk about it, but the women work most for it.

<div align="right">FRANCES WATKINS HARPER</div>

◈

Just break the news to mother,
 She knows how dear I love her,
And tell her not to wait for me,
 For I'm not coming home.

<div align="right">CHARLES K. HARRIS</div>

◈

The commonest fallacy among women is that simply having children makes one a mother—which is absurd as believing that having a piano makes one a musician.

<div align="right">SYDNEY J. HARRIS</div>

◈

Everybody knows that a good mother gives her children a feeling of trust and stability. She is their earth. . . Only to touch her skirt or her sleeve makes a troubled child feel better.

Mother is the one we count on for the things that matter most of all.

<div align="right">KATHERINE BUTLER HATHAWAY</div>

The successful mother sets her children free and becomes more free herself in the process.

<div align="right">ROBERT J. HAVIGHURST</div>

≈

Before you were conceived I wanted you
Before you were born I loved you
Before you were here an hour I would die for you.
This is the miracle of life.

<div align="right">MAUREEN HAWKINS</div>

≈

What is home without a mother?

<div align="right">ALICE HAWTHORNE</div>

≈

Back of every achievement is a proud wife and a surprised mother-in-law.

<div align="right">BROOKS HAYS</div>

≈

My mother was dead for five years before I knew that I loved her very much.

<div align="right">LILLIAN HELLMAN</div>

≈

There is none,
In all this cold and hollow world, no fount
Of deep, strong, deathless love, save that within
A mother's heart.

<div align="right">FELICIA D. HEMANS</div>

The toughest part of motherhood is the inner worrying and not showing it.

AUDREY HEPBURN

❧

Among the things a mother should tell her daughter is never to trust a man to remember to water the geranium.

HERALD (WINTER HAVEN, FLORIDA NEWSPAPER)

❧

Other people's babies—
That's my life!
Mother to dozens,
And nobody's wife.

A. P. HERBERT

❧

He that wipes the child's nose kisseth the mother's cheek.

GEORGE HERBERT

❧

The most important thing a father can do for his children is to love their mother.

THEODORE M. HESBURGH

❧

Youth fades; love droops, the leaves of friendship fall; A mother's secret hope outlives them all.

The real religion of the world comes from woman much more than from men—from mothers most of all, who carry the key of our souls in their bosoms.

<div align="right">OLIVER WENDELL HOLMES</div>

ð

Thus she spoke; and I longed to embrace my dead mother's ghost. Thrice I tried to clasp her image and thrice it slipped through my hands, like a shadow, like a dream.

<div align="right">HOMER</div>

ð

. . . my mother is soothed at first by her television, watching lives much more professional than ours.

<div align="right">MAUREEN HOWARD</div>

ð

A man never sees all that his mother has been to him till it's too late to let her know that he sees it.

<div align="right">WILLIAM DEAN HOWELLS</div>

ð

The headliner in God's great vaudeville.

<div align="right">ELBERT HUBBARD</div>

ð

Behind every successful man stands a surprised mother-in-law.

<div align="right">HUBERT HUMPHREY</div>

The florists are everywhere the most ardent of matriolaters.

ALDOUS HUXLEY

❧

A man loves his sweetheart the most, his wife the best, but his mother the longest.

IRISH PROVERB

❧

A father may turn his back on his child; brothers and sisters may become inveterate enemies; husbands may desert their wives, and wives their husbands. But a mother's love endures through all.

A mother's love endures through all; in good repute, in the face of the world's condemnation, a mother still loves on and still hopes that her child may turn from his evil ways, and repent.

A mother is the truest friend we have, when trials, heavy and sudden, fall upon us; when adversity takes the place of prosperity; when friends who rejoice with us in our sunshine, desert us when troubles thicken around us, still will she cling to us, and endeavor by her kind precepts and counsels to dissipate the clouds of darkness, and cause peace to return to our hearts.

WASHINGTON IRVING

❧

This is a child who is always crying.
Be quiet, my soul, for mother is coming back.
She will bring thee nice milk
And then put thee in the crib to hushaby.

ITALIAN LULLABY

Motherhood is priced
Of God, at price no man may dare
To lessen or misunderstand.

HELEN HUNT JACKSON

❧

A mother never realizes that her children are no longer children.

HOLBROOK JACKSON

❧

Mothers make men.

THOMAS JEFFERSON

❧

But there, everything, has its drawbacks, as the man said when his mother-in-law died, and they came down upon him for the funeral expenses.

JEROME K. JEROME

❧

You never get over being a child, 'long as you have a mother to go to.

SARAH ORNE JEWETT

❧

God could not be everywhere and therefore He made mothers.

A woman doesn't mind her son becoming a boxer as long as he becomes a doctor or lawyer first.

JEWISH SAYING

In general those parents have the most reverence deserve it.

<div align="right">SAMUEL JOHNSON</div>

❧

Now, as always, the most automated appliance in a household is a mother.

<div align="right">BEVERLY JONES</div>

❧

A mother is a person who seeing there are only four pieces of pie for five people, promptly announces she never did care for pie.

<div align="right">TENNEVA JORDAN</div>

❧

A certain grandma was so delighted when she heard that her grandchildren were coming for a visit that she gave five dollars to the church. The following Sunday, after the children had left, she gave ten dollars.

<div align="right">JOURNAL (WASHINGTON, IOWA NEWSPAPER)</div>

❧

Whatever else is unsure in this stinking dunghill of a world a mother's love is not.

<div align="right">JAMES JOYCE</div>

❧

. . . creative work grows out of the unconscious depths, indeed out of the region of the mother.

<div align="right">CARL GUSTAV JUNG</div>

Mothers all want their sons to grow up to be president, but they don't want them to become politicians in the process.

JOHN F. KENNEDY

૨ð

I would much rather be known as the mother of a great son than the author of a great book or the painter of a great masterpiece.

I looked on child rearing not only as a work of love and duty but as a profession that was fully as interesting and challenging as any honorable profession in the world and one that demanded the best that I could bring it.

ROSE KENNEDY

૨ð

The socially pernicious, racially wasteful, and soul-withering consequences of the working of mothers outside the home must cease. And this can only come to pass, either through the programme of institutional upbringing or through the intimated renaissance of the home.

ELLEN KEY

૨ð

When people inquire I always just state, "I have four nice children, and hope to have eight."

ALINE MURRAY KILMER

૨ð

Sometimes the strength of motherhood is greater than natural laws.

BARBARA KINGSOLVER

Now in memory comes my mother,
 As she used, in years agone,
To regard the darling dreamers
 Ere she left them till the dawn.

COATES KINNEY

ॐ

If I were damned of body and soul,
I know whose prayers would make me whole,
Mother o' mine, O mother o' mine!

RUDYARD KIPLING

ॐ

Mother's love grows by giving.

CHARLES LAMB

ॐ

Children are what the mother are; no fondest father's fondest
care can so fashion the infant's heart or so shape the life.

WALTER SAVAGE LANDOR

ॐ

A timid man's mother does not weep (having no fear for her
son's safety).

LATIN PROVERB

ॐ

She seems to have had the ability to stand firmly on the rock
of her past while living completely and unregretfully in the
present.

MADELEINE L'ENGLE

All that I am or hope to be I owe to my mother.

No man is poor who has a godly mother.

ABRAHAM LINCOLN

ॐ

I have often wished for the blessing of motherhood for it would have given me a much needed focal point for my affections. With it and through the various experiences that accompany it, I could perhaps have achieved something better than that which I have attained up to now.

JENNY LIND

ॐ

On earth you will ne'er have another,
In this weary world there's no other,
And God only gives you one mother!
So cherish and love her most dear.

JENNIE LINDAY

ॐ

By and large, mothers and housewives are the only workers who do not have regular time off. They are the great vacationless class.

ANNE MORROW LINDBERGH

ॐ

Motherhood is so honorable a thing that nothing—no convention—can possibly make it dishonorable.

BEN B. LINDSEY AND WAINWRIGHT EVANS

Of course, everybody knows that the greatest thing about Motherhood is the "Sacrifices," but it is quite a shock to find out that they begin so far ahead of time.

<div align="right">ANITA LOOS</div>

When you are a mother, you are never really alone in your thoughts. You are connected to your child and to all those who touch your lives. A mother always has to think twice, once for herself and once for her child.

Is my mother my friend? I would have to say, first of all she is my Mother, with a capital 'M'; she's something sacred to me. I love her dearly . . . yes, she is also a good friend, someone I can talk openly with if I want to.

<div align="right">SOPHIA LOREN</div>

Life was diapers and little jars of pureed apricots and bottles and playpens and rectal thermometers and all those small dirty faces and all those questions.

<div align="right">PAT LOUD</div>

Many make a household but only one the home.

The best academy, a mother's knee.

<div align="right">JAMES RUSSELL LOWELL</div>

There is nothing sweeter than the heart of a pious mother.

<div align="right">MARTIN LUTHER</div>

You may have friends, fond, dear friends, but never will you have again the inexpressible love and gentleness lavished upon you, which none but a mother bestows.

THOMAS B. MACAULAY

૨ঌ

A mother of seventeen children says that having another child is the only way she knows to keep the youngest child from being spoiled.

MADISON PRESS (LONDON, OHIO NEWSPAPER)

૨ঌ

In the dark womb where I began
My mother's life made me a man.
Through all the months of human birth
Her beauty fed my common earth
I cannot see, nor breathe, nor stir
But through the death of some of her.

JOHN MASEFIELD

૨ঌ

I would weave you a song, my mother, . . .
Yours the tender hand Upon my breast;
Yours the voice Sounding ever in my ears.

MADELEINE MASON-MANHEIM

૨ঌ

Few misfortunes can befall a boy which bring worse consequences than to have a really affectionate mother.

W. SOMERSET MAUGHAM

Your love for your mother is something that you never completely comprehend until you are separated by the miles from her warmth and her wonder.

COLLIN McCARTY

&

A mother's hardest to forgive.
Life is the fruit she longs to hand to you.
Ripe on a plate. And while you live,
Relentlessly she understands you.

PHYLLIS McGINLEY

&

One of the oldest human needs is having someone to wonder where you are when you don't come home at night.

MARGARET MEAD

&

It is only in our advanced and synthetic civilization that mothers no longer sing to the babies they are carrying.

YEHUDI MENUHIN

&

My hands are too tired to hold a torch on high, but they can light a candle in a nursery.

ELLIS MEREDITH

&

There is another mistake I forgot to mention usual in mothers. If any of their daughters are beauties, they take great pains to persuade them that they are ugly.

LADY MARY WORTLEY MONTAGU

This heart, my own dear mother, bends,
With love's true instinct, back to thee.

THOMAS MOORE

❧

Every beetle is a gazelle in the eyes of its mother.

MOORISH PROVERB

❧

When a man's mother holds his child in her gladdened arms he is aware . . . of the roundness of life's cycle; of the mystic harmony of life's way.

A man's mother is so tissued and woven into his life and brain that he can no more describe her than describe the air and sunlight that bless his days.

To walk and talk with them is like slipping on an old coat. To hear their voices is like the shake of music in a sober evening hush.

CHRISTOPHER MORLEY

❧

I never knew
My Mother's words
Which I thought dull, didactical,
Would prove in time,
As decades sped,
So right, so sound, so practical!

LOIS MUEHL

The future destiny of the child is always the work of the mother.

NAPOLEON

ठ

Children aren't happy with nothing to ignore, And that's what parents were created for.

OGDEN NASH

ठ

One moment makes a father, but a mother is made by endless moments, load on load.

JOHN C. NEIHARDT

ठ

. . . she did not understand how her father could have reached such an age and such eminence without learning that all mothers are as infallible as any pope and more righteous than any saint.

FRANCES NEWMAN

ठ

Medical researchers can't realistically expect to find a cure quicker than Mom kissing the place that hurts.

NEWS (KELLOGY, IDAHO NEWSPAPER)

ठ

A smart father teaches his son how to make money, because he knows that somewhere a smart mother is teaching her daughter how to spend it happily.

NEWS-BLADE (BRIDGEPORT, NEBRASKA NEWSPAPER)

The mother of several children who goes out for the afternoon without taking one of them with her looks like the most relaxed person in the world for an hour or so. Then she begins to look worried.

NEWS-CHAMPION (GUNNISOM, COLORADO NEWSPAPER)

❧

I don't think that all good mothers have to bake and sew and make beds and wear percale bungalow aprons. Some of the finest never go into their kitchens at all; some of the most devoted are also some of the richest.

KATHLEEN NORRIS

❧

Clearly, society has a tremendous stake in insisting on a woman's natural fitness for the career of mother: the alternatives are all too expensive.

ANN OAKLEY

❧

If you bungle raising your children, I don't think whatever else you do well matters very much.

JACQUELINE KENNEDY ONASSIS

❧

With more fortitude does a mother long for one out of many, than she who weeping cries, "Thou wast my only one."

OVID

Every man must define his identity against his mother. If he does not, he just falls back into her and is swallowed up.

CAMILLE PAGLIA

ઠ

Nothing else will ever make you as happy or as sad, as proud or as tired, as motherhood.

ELIA PARSONS

ઠ

One scream of fear from a mother may resound through the whole life of her daughter.

JEAN PAUL

ઠ

Heaven is at the feet of mothers.

PERSIAN PROVERB

ઠ

One race there is of men, one of gods, but from one mother we both draw our breaths.

PINDAR

ઠ

Intolerable . . . is the abuse whereby mothers of families, because of the insufficiency of the father's salary, are forced to engage in gainful occupations outside the domestics walls to the neglect of their own proper cares and duties, particularly the education of their children.

PIUS XI (ACHILLE AMBROGIO DAMIANO)

The angels . . . singing unto one another,
Can find among their burning terms of love,
None so devotional as that of "mother."

EDGAR ALLAN POE

The greatest love is a mother's, then a dog's, then a sweet-heart's.

POLISH PROVERB

Every mother is like Moses. She does not enter the promised land. She prepares a world she will not see.

POPE PAUL VI

A diligent mother, a lazy daughter.

PORTUGUESE PROVERB

Who has not watched a mother stroke her child's cheek or kiss her child *in a certain way,* and felt a nervous shudder at the possessive outrage done to a free solitary human soul?

JOHN COWPER POWYS

The mother who can manage her children with dispatch can get them ready and sent to play with the youngster next door before the youngsters there can get to her house.

PRESS (ST. CHARLES, MINNESOTA NEWSPAPER)

Being pregnant is . . . an occupational hazard of being a wife.

PRINCESS ANNE

With animals you don't see the male caring for the offspring. It's against nature. It's a woman's prerogative and duty, and a privilege.

PRINCESS GRACE OF MONACO

A mother-in-law dies only when another devil is needed in hell.

FRANÇOIS RABELAIS

A mother has an innate ability for aggravating the wounds of her offspring's pride. This is inevitable since the relationship between mother and child is a most unnatural one; other species have the good sense to banish their young at an early age.

JOHN RAE

Romance fails us and so do friendships—but the relationship of mother and child remains indelible and indestructible—the strongest bond on this earth.

THEODOR REIK

I opine . . . "Judicious mothers will always keep in mind, that they are the first book read, and the last put aside, in every child's library."

C. LENOX REMOND

Oh, to be only half as wonderful as my child thought I was when he was small, and only half as stupid as my teen-ager now thinks I am.

REBECCA RICHARDS

❧

No joy in nature is so sublimely affecting as the joy of a mother at the good fortune of her child.

JEAN PAUL RICHTER

❧

Give her a day, and then in return Momma gives you the other 364. See?

I doubt if a charging elephant, or a rhino, is as determined or hard to check as a socially ambitious mother.

Mothers are the only race of people that speak the same tongue. A mother in Manchuria could converse with a mother in Nebraska and never miss a word.

WILL ROGERS

❧

I think, at a child's birth, if a mother could ask a fairy god-mother to endow it with the most useful gift, that gift would be curiosity.

ELEANOR ROOSEVELT

❧

The mother is the one supreme asset of national life; she is more important by far than the successful statesman, or businessman, or artist, or scientist.

Into a woman's keeping is committed the destiny of the generations to come.

THEODORE ROOSEVELT

❧

Only in America . . . do these peasants, our mothers, get their hair dyed platinum at the age of sixty, and walk up and down Collins Avenue in Florida in pedal pushers and mink stoles—and with opinions on every subject under the sun. It isn't their fault that they were given a gift like speech—look if cows could talk they would say things just as idiotic.

PHILIP ROTH

❧

The true mother, far from being a woman of the world, is as much a recluse in her home as the nun is in her cloister.

The mother breast-fed her children at first for her own sake; and afterwards, when habit endeared them to her, for theirs.

JEAN JACQUES ROUSSEAU

❧

What tigress is there that does not purr over her young ones and fawn upon them in tenderness?

ST. AUGUSTINE

❧

A mother loves her children even when they least deserve to be loved.

KATE SAMPERI

No woman can call herself free until she can choose consciously whether she will or will not be a mother.

Awaken the womanhood of America to free the motherhood of the world!

When motherhood becomes the fruit of a deep yearning, not the result of ignorance or accident, its children will become the foundation of a new race.

MARGARET SANGER

&

Why isn't more said about the sensuousness between mother and baby? Men paint it and seem to assume it—women don't even mention it among themselves. Either it is completely taken for granted or it isn't considered at all. It's more than a fringe benefit.

FRANCES KARLEN SANTAMARIA

&

The ideal mother, like the ideal marriage, is a fiction.

It is impossible for a woman to love her children twenty-four hours a day.

MILTON R. SAPIRSTEIN

&

Hesperus, you herd homeward whatever Dawn's light dispersed: you herd sheep—herd goats—her children home to their mother.

SAPPHO

Children reinvent your world for you.

SUSAN SARANDON

A mother understands what a child does not say.

SAYING

Never rely on the glory of the morning or on the smile of your mother-in-law.

J. W. R. SCOTT

O hush thee, my babie, thy sire was a knight,
Thy mother a lady, both lovely and bright.

SIR WALTER SCOTT

No matter how old a mother is, she watches her middle-aged children for signs of improvement.

FLORIDA SCOTT-MAXWELL

A mother never gets hit by a custard pie. Mothers-in-law—yes. But mothers—never.

MACK SENNETT

My mother is everywhere . . .
In the perfume of a rose,
The eyes of a tiger,
The pages of a book,
The food we partake,
The whistling wind of the desert,
The blazing gems of sunset,
The crystal light of full moon,
The opal veils of sunrise.

GRACE SETON-THOMPSON

೩

So loving to my mother
That he might not beteem the winds of heaven
Visit her face too roughly.

 Thou hast never in thy life
Show'd thy dear mother any courtesy;
When she—poor hen! fond of no second brood—
Has cluck'd thee to the wars, and safely home,
Loaden with honour.

Thou art thy mother's glass, and she in thee
Calls back the lovely April of her prime.

Macduff was from his mother's womb
Untimely ripp'd.

(Motherhood) The pleasing punishment that women bear.

O wonderful son, that can so astonish a mother!

And all my mother came into mine eyes
And gave me up to tears.

Her voice was ever soft,
Gentle and low, an excellent thing in woman.

WILLIAM SHAKESPEARE

❧

Of all human struggles there is none so treacherous and re-
morseless as the struggle between the artist man and the mother
woman.

GEORGE B. SHAW

❧

Observe how soon, and to what a degree, a mother's influence
begins to operate! Her first ministration for her infant is to enter,
as it were, the valley of the shadow of death, and win its life at the
peril of her own! How different must an affection thus founded
be from all others!

LYDIA H. SIGOURNEY

❧

One pill makes you taller
And one pill makes you small
And the ones that mother gives you
Don't do anything at all.

GRACE SLICK

❧

Do not join encounter groups. If you enjoy being made to feel
inadequate, call your mother.

LIZ SMITH

Oh! when a Mother meets on high
The Babe she lost in infancy,
Hath she not then, for pains and fears,
The day of woe, the watchful night,
Sons are the anchors of a Mother's life.

SOPHOCLES

For all her sorrow, all her tears,
An overpayment of delight.

ROBERT SOUTHEY

Women are aristocrats, and it is always the mother who makes us feel that we belong to the better sort.

JOHN LANCASTER SPALDING

An ounce of mother is worth a pound of clergy.

SPANISH PROVERB

I really learned it all from mothers.

The more people have studied different methods of bringing up children the more they have come to the conclusion that what good mothers and fathers instinctively feel like doing for their babies is the best after all.

DR. BENJAMIN SPOCK

Though motherhood is the most important of all the professions—requiring more knowledge than any other depart in human affairs—there was no attention given to preparation for this office.

Parents can never do too much for their children to repay them for the injustice of having brought them into the world, unless they have insured them high moral and intellectual gifts, fine physical health and enough money and education to render life something more than one ceaseless struggle for necessities.

ELIZABETH CADY STANTON

&

It's clear that most American children suffer too much mother and too little father.

GLORIA STEINEM

&

Making the decision to have a child—it's momentous. It is to decide forever to have your heart go walking around outside your body.

ELIZABETH STONE

&

. . . these remarkable women of olden times are like the ancient painted glass—the art of making them is lost; my mother was less than her mother, and I am less than my mother.

Mothers are the most instinctive philosophers.

HARRIET BEECHER STOWE

The world has no such flower in any land,
And no such pearl in any gulf the sea
As any babe on any mother's knee.

Mother, thou sole and only, thou not these,
Keep me in mind a little when I die,
Because I was thy first born. . .

A. C. SWINBURNE

&

Who ran to help me when I fell
And would some pretty story tell,
Or kiss the part to make it well?
My mother.

ANN TAYLOR

&

A spoilt child never loves its mother.

HENRY TAYLOR

&

Mothers soften their children with kisses and imperfect noises, with the pap and breastmilk of soft endearments; they rescue them from tutors, and snatch them from discipline, they desire to keep them fat and warm, and their feet dry, and their bellies full, and then the children govern, and cry, and prove fools and troublesome.

JEREMY TAYLOR

Happy he
With such a mother! faith in womankind
Beats with his blood, and truth in all things high
Comes easy to him.

ALFRED, LORD TENNYSON

≈

Is not a young mother one of the sweetest sights which life
shows us?

WILLIAM THACKERAY

≈

Be a stepmother kindly as she will,
There's in her love some hint of winter's chill.

D'ARCY W. THOMPSON

≈

Her own mother lived the latter years of her life in the horri-
ble suspicion that electricity was dripping invisibly all over the
house.

JAMES THURBER

≈

My mother had a great deal of trouble with me, but I think she
enjoyed it.

It is at our mother's knee that we acquire our noblest and truest
and highest ideals.

MARK TWAIN

If you want your children to turn out well, spend twice as much time with them, and half as much money.

ABIGAIL VAN BUREN

I knew what I had to have before my soul would rest. I wanted to belong—to belong to my mother. And in return—I wanted my mother to belong to me.

GLORIA VANDERBILT

Being a full-time mother is one of the highest salaried jobs . . . since the payment is pure love.

MILDRED B. VERMONT

Begin, little boy, to recognize your mother by a smile.

VIRGIL

My best creation is my children.

DIANE VON FURSTENBURG

We have a beautiful
Mother
Her green lap
immense
Her brown embrace
eternal
Her blue body
everything
we know.

<div align="right">ALICE WALKER</div>

≥≈

For the hand that rocks the cradle
Is the hand that rules the world.

<div align="right">WILLIAM ROSS WALLACE</div>

≥≈

I attribute all my success in life to the moral, intellectual and
physical education which I received from my mother.

<div align="right">GEORGE WASHINGTON</div>

≥≈

I was not a classic mother. But my kids were never palmed off
to boarding school. So, I didn't bake cookies. You can buy cook-
ies, but you can't buy love.

<div align="right">RAQUEL WELCH</div>

Motherhood is the strangest thing, it can be like being one's own Trojan horse.

<div align="right">REBECCA WEST</div>

ð⊾

Ah. lucky girls who grow up in the shelter of a mother's love — a mother who knows how to contrive opportunities without conceding favors, how to take advantage of propinquity without allowing appetite to be dulled by habit.

<div align="right">EDITH WHARTON</div>

ð⊾

To her, the ideal woman, practical, spiritual, of all of earth, life, love, to me the best.

> . . . Where the city of the best-bodied mothers stands
> There the great city stands.

<div align="right">WALT WHITMAN</div>

ð⊾

Most of all the other beautiful things in life come by twos and threes by dozens and hundreds. Plenty of roses, stars, sunsets, rainbows, brothers, and sisters, aunts and cousins, but only one mother in the whole world.

<div align="right">KATE DOUGLAS WIGGIN</div>

ð⊾

The American girl is taught that she is a young princess from her cradle to the altar. It is a great misfortune when she forgets that the mother of a princess must be a queen . . . and should so be treated.

<div align="right">ELLA WHEELER WILCOX</div>

Children begin by loving their parents. After a time, they judge them. Rarely, if ever, do they forgive them.

All women become like their mothers. That is their tragedy. No man does. That is his.

<div align="right">OSCAR WILDE</div>

æ

My father got me strong and straight and slim
And I give thanks to him.
My mother bore me glad and sound and sweet
I kiss her feet!

<div align="right">MARGUERITE WILKINSON</div>

æ

Biology is the least of what makes someone a mother.

<div align="right">OPRAH WINFREY</div>

æ

The most remarkable thing about a mother is her ability to be hurt so much by her baby and to hate so much without paying the child out, and her ability to wait for rewards that may or may not come at a later date.

<div align="right">D. W. WINNICOTT</div>

æ

The neglected wife is, in general, the best mother.

<div align="right">MARY WOLLSTONECRAFT</div>

Mama was my greatest teacher, a teacher of compassion, love and fearlessness. If love is sweet as a flower, then my mother is that sweet flower of love.

<div align="right">STEVIE WONDER</div>

Years to a mother bring distress,
But do not make her love the less.

Thou, while thy babes around thee cling,
Shalt show us how divine a thing
A woman may be made.

<div align="right">WILLIAM WORDSWORTH</div>

A mother becomes a true grandmother the day she stops noticing the terrible things her children do because she is so enchanted with the wonderful things her grandchildren do.

<div align="right">LOIS WYSE</div>

Of all the rights of women, the greatest is to be a mother.

<div align="right">LIN YUTANG</div>